DAVID
The Brave Shepherd Boy Who Became a Great King
Retold by Ben Alex
Illustrated by François Davot
© Copyright 1988 by Scandinavia
Publishing House, Nørregade 32, DK-1165 Copenhagen K.
English-language edition published 1989
through special arrangement with Scandinavia
by Wm. B. Eerdmans Publishing Co.,
255 Jefferson Ave. S.E., Grand Rapids, Michigan 49503
All rights reserved
Printed in Hong Kong
ISBN 0-8028-5031-6

2

David

The Brave Shepherd Boy Who Became a Great King

Retold by Ben Alex
Illustrated by François Davot

Eerdmans

It was lovely in the green hills outside Bethlehem.

From the top of the hill where the shepherd boy sat, he could see many miles away. Below, the lush fields lay like a great carpet over the valley. Off to the right, the houses of Bethlehem were clustered around the marketplace. They looked like a heap of square rocks in the sunshine. To the left the sheep spread out, grazing on the slope below.

Suddenly a shout broke the silence of the hills and echoed throughout the valley, "David! David!"

The shepherd boy spun around. He had a tanned face, sparkling dark eyes, black curly hair, and strong limbs. His brother Eliab came running up the hill.

"David! Hurry back home!"

"Why? Is anything wrong?" asked David, waiting for his brother to catch his breath.

"You'll . . . have to . . . come . . . right away!" Eliab panted. "Samuel, the prophet, has come to visit."

"What? Why would Samuel come to Bethlehem? Who's in trouble?"

"It could be you!" answered Eliab. "Samuel wants to see you!" Whenever Samuel wanted to see people it usually meant they had sinned and were in trouble.

David's eyes bulged in surprise. "Why me?"

Eliab explained, "I don't know. The prophet just looked at each one of us. Then he shook his head and asked Jesse, our father, 'Don't you have any more sons?' So Father sent me to fetch you!"

Eliab turned and galloped off down the hill. David followed close at his heels.

David's seven brothers stood lined up in the farmyard. In front of them, the famous prophet Samuel was leaning on his staff. Nobody said a word. They all were waiting for David.

"Here he comes!" exclaimed Jesse.

David slipped into the end of the line. Being the youngest, he was used to being last and being teased and talked down to. "You're

only a child!" his brothers often taunted. Then they would tickle him or laugh behind his back. Sometimes they called him nasty names and then knocked him on the back of the head. How David hated it! He longed to grow up and become big like his brothers. But today they did not tease him. They just wondered what terrible things he had done to deserve a visit from Samuel.

David wondered the same. Why did Samuel the prophet want to see him?

Samuel's piercing eyes fell upon David. He squinted, then a trace of a smile brightened his eyes.

"He's the one!" Samuel's hoarse voice announced.

David began to tremble. "Which one?" he mumbled. Then he saw Samuel pull out a bull horn and fill it with oil. The prophet was going to anoint somebody! In Israel a man was anointed with oil when he was to be used by God in a special way. The last person Samuel had anointed was King Saul.

Surprise filled the eyes of David's older brothers. Did it mean one of them was to become a disciple of Samuel or some other kind of important leader?

Samuel poured the holy oil over David's head. Everybody held his breath. David was thinking, "Why me? I'm only a shepherd boy." David's brothers were thinking the same thing.

The oldest brother, Eliab, thought, "I'm older and stronger than David."

The next brother, Abinadab, thought, "I'm smarter than David."

The next brother, Shammah, thought, "I'm better looking." Each of Jesse's sons had a good reason for thinking he should be the one to be anointed instead of David.

But Samuel did not even give them a second glance. He just nodded goodbye to Jesse and said, "The Lord doesn't look at the outside of someone. He looks at the heart." Then he turned on his heel and left as suddenly as he had come.

As David went back to his flock of sheep, his brothers stared after him. Their youngest brother had been anointed by the prophet, chosen by God to become His special servant! How could this be?

F. DAVOT

At that time there were rumors of war in the land of Israel. Some people said the Philistines were gathering an army to fight against Israel. Israel had known many enemies, but the Philistines were the worst.

David's three oldest brothers, Eliab, Abinadab, and Shammah, were soldiers in the army of Israel. Sometimes they came home on leave and talked about how proud they were to be soldiers.

"Now tell me," said Jesse during one of their visits, "is it true what they say about the king? I've heard he has become grumpy and moody. They say his own family is afraid of him. Some even say he has gone crazy."

"There's something to it, father," Eliab said sadly. "King Saul is suspicious and jealous of everyone. Nobody is safe around him anymore."

"Yes," continued Abinadab. "He sits for days and stares into space. The morale of the soldiers is getting worse and worse."

Jesse sighed. "I wonder what's going to become of Israel? Things are not what they used to be."

"Just leave it to us, father," said Shammah. "We are soldiers now. We'll crush the Philistines."

"I want to become a soldier, too," beamed David. He loved to listen to his brothers' reports from the battlefield. However, he had to stay home and take care of his father's sheep.

"Sure," laughed the brothers, "you're still just a baby."

"Hey dreamer," they added. "Made up any new sheep songs lately?"

That same morning, as David was playing his lyre in the hayloft, there was a pounding on the gate. It was a messenger from King Saul himself with a request for Jesse. Jesse could hardly believe his own ears.

"The king requests your youngest son, David, to come right away to the palace and make music for the king."

David was scared and excited at the same time. As he left, his seven brothers stood at the gate, scratching their heads. David, their youngest brother, requested by the king? Now they were not laughing.

"Bye," smiled David. Then he rode off with the king's messenger.

K ing Saul sat on his throne and waited for the new musician. His General Abner had advised Saul to listen to good music. "It would make you feel better," Abner assured him.

Saul did not even notice when David entered the room. He just sat there and stared into space. His eyes were lifeless. He looked tired and worried. His face was pale like that of a dead man. David cleared his throat and began to sing.

The music filled the rooms of the royal palace as it had the hills of Bethlehem. It spoke of the quietness of the fields, the simple life of the shepherd, the happiness of those who put their trust in God.

David trusted God. Even though he had often wondered what it was that God had chosen him for, he was patiently waiting for God to lead him.

Slowly Saul's eyes began to brighten. Color and expression returned to his pale face. He turned toward the new musician and whispered hoarsely, "Go on! I like that!"

David continued, "The Lord is my Shepherd, I shall not want. . . . " The music was like weightless butterflies fluttering in the king's room.

From then on, Saul often asked David to play the lyre and sing for him. He started to look much better. He even began to smile. He had guests come eat around his table. Then, suddenly, the happy days came to an end.

Runners arrived from the valley of Elah. "The Philistine army has marched into the other side of the valley," they reported. "They could attack any time. Saul, you are needed to lead your men."

So, Saul hurried off to his army at Elah.

And David returned to his home in Bethlehem.

David liked being back home. He had missed his sheep and the hills where he made his songs and talked to God. But he often thought back to the time when he had played for King Saul. He dreamed the king would someday send for him again. He still did not realize that God was preparing him for something more.

Each evening at sunset, when David brought his flock of sheep back to the sheepfold, the sheep would crowd through the narrow opening in the stone wall. David called each one by name. Then, when all were safe inside, he would spread his skin mattress in front of the doorway and lie watching the stars before he fell asleep. He became the door to the sheepfold. No one could come in and harm his lambs. Until one night. . . .

"Grrraaaaugh!" It was a frightening roar!

David shot three feet into the air and landed on his feet. For a moment he stood paralyzed. Only his eyes moved. S-l-o-w-l-y he turned his head and looked right into the eyes of a . . . lion!

The animal stood on top of the stone wall. Its huge body was bathed in the moonlight. David had goose bumps all over, even in his hair. In a minute the lion would jump down and devour either him or one of his lambs. Without a sound David reached down and searched with his hand for his rod. He did not take his eyes off the lion for even a second. And then. . . .

David shot into the air like a cat going for its prey. He landed on the back of the lion and forced the rod towards the soft point under the lion's throat, pulling with all his might. The lion stiffened for a second. It growled once, then collapsed, limp as a rag. It slid down the wall and rolled over on its side.

It was dead! David had broken the lion's neck!

That night it took a long time for David to fall asleep. "Thank You, God," he whispered. "I know I couldn't have done this by myself. Thank You for giving me strength to kill the lion!"

At breakfast the next morning David told his family what had happened. His brothers shook their heads doubtfully, "Killed a lion? David? How would he do something like that?" They chuckled under their breath. They had sometimes believed his stories about killing bears. But he had killed them from a distance with his slingshot. After all, David was good with a sling. They could admit that. But breaking the neck of a lion? That was beyond belief.

"It wasn't really me," said David. "God did it."

"God?" laughed his brothers. But when they went outside to examine the dead lion on the ground, they stopped laughing. Without saying another word, they went off to work.

Jesse was proud of his youngest son. "Well done, David!" he exclaimed. "You deserve a day off. I want you to go to where your other brothers are stationed at Elah. They'll be needing some more food. Look for them in the front line of King Saul's army."

"Oh, I was hoping you'd say that, father!" shouted David as he lifted his father up in the air. He could hardly wait to see the king's army for himself.

King Saul's army was lined up on the eastern slope of the valley of Elah. The Philistine army was posted on the western slope. But what a difference! The Israelites looked more like farmers out on a hunt than soldiers at war. Only a few of them had any real armor or weapons. Most Israelites carried rods and homemade stone weapons. But the Philistine army carried iron weapons and shields. They wore bronze helmets.

David elbowed his way through the rods and spears and legs of his countrymen. He wanted to see his three brothers on the front line. Suddenly someone hit him on the back of his head. He swayed and spun around.

"David! What are you doing here? This is the king's army! Aren't you supposed to be tending sheep?" Eliab looked angry.

"Father sent me . . ."

"Don't make things up," interrupted Abinadab. "You came to watch the battle,

didn't you?" Then he grabbed David by the shoulder and pushed him. David staggered three steps backwards and landed flat on his back.

"Can't I even explain?" he yelled. "I'm your brother. I've come with supplies for you, and you treat me like dirt!" Then he stood up and walked off.

Just at that moment something happened which made the entire army of Israel tremble in their sandals. David stopped and stared.

A soldier emerged from the ranks of the Philistine army. He was huge! Absolutely gigantic! David stopped breathing as he watched him. The giant walked out into the middle of the valley and stopped. He looked like an enormous bronze statue with helmet and full-scale coat of armor. A bronze javelin was slung across his back. In his hand he held a spear the size of a boat mast. His shield bearer standing at his side looked like a dwarf in comparison.

F. DAVOT

"All that must weigh at least two hundred pounds!" gasped David. He turned to the nearest Israelite. "Who is this man? Has he come out to fight all by himself?"

"He's Goliath from Gath," stammered the Israelite soldier. "The Philistines think we should settle this war with a contest between the giant and an Israelite. For the last forty days he has come out to challenge us. But nobody dares fight against him."

"I don't blame them," mumbled David.

David kept his eye on the giant. The man looked like a monster, not a human being, he was so tall! Then the giant lifted his arm. The Israelites shivered as he bellowed, "Listen, you slaves of Israel! Where is the man who wants to fight me? If he can kill me, we'll all surrender to you. But if I kill him, you must surrender to us." Then Goliath thumbed his nose at the Israelites and yelled, "Today I defy the ranks of Israel!"

David was shocked! His chin dropped. His knuckles went white, he clenched his shepherd's rod so tightly. He could not believe anyone would dare defy the people of God. David's eyes riveted onto the giant as he said slowly but firmly, "Will somebody bring me before the king? I'll fight the giant!"

King Saul looked at David. He did not recognize his former musician. Then he looked at the giant. A wry smile crept over his face. "You can't fight the giant," the king said. "You don't even know what you're doing."

David tried to ignore Saul's words. "I'm not afraid of that ungodly Philistine!" he answered.

"How old are you?" the king asked.

"I'm sixteen. Sixteen-and-a-half."

"And you want me to believe you can fight giants?"

"I've killed bears and lions before!"

King Saul thought for a minute. Then he said, "All right, go ahead. You may fight the Philistine since nobody else will."

F. DAVOT

Saul insisted David put on his own royal armor. He loaded his weapons into David's hands. David looked like a little boy playing soldier. The king's helmet kept falling down over his eyes.

"This won't work," David finally said. "I'll fight the giant my way!" He took off the royal armor. Then he went to meet Goliath from Gath.

But his brothers were angry. They stared after him as if to say, "That's it! See now, what this crazy little brother of ours has got us into!"

But David kneeled down and picked up five smooth stones. Then he pulled out the sling from his belt. In the other hand he held his rod and walked down into the valley.

Now it was the giant's turn to be shocked. "What do you think I am?" he shouted at David. "A dog? I asked for a proper soldier, and out steps a shepherd lad armed with a rod! I'll turn you into vulture food!"

Goliath took three giant steps forward. "That's what you think!" David yelled back. "You come against me with all your fancy armor. But I come against you in the name of the Lord! He is the God of the army of Israel whom you've defied. Today the Lord will give you into my hands!"

David was only fifty feet away from the giant. He reached into his bag, took out a stone, and placed it in the sling. Taking aim at the giant's forehead, right between the eyes, he pictured the stone smashing through Goliath's skull.

"God," he whispered, "help me aim steady and make my stone fly straight." Then he whirled the sling over his head and sent the stone whining through the air.

"Smack!" The stone hurled through the air and was right on target. For a minute Goliath tottered cross-eyed. Then he gave a yelp, stumbled forward and thudded onto the ground like some giant tree trunk. "Whommm!"

David could feel the ground shake beneath his feet.

There was total silence. The soldiers on both sides tiptoed forward to find out what had happened. David ran straight up to Goliath and pulled out the giant's sword. He raised it high over his head.

"Zaapppp!" The giant's head went rolling.

David grasped it by the hair and held it up in the air. Suddenly the eastern side of the valley turned into a tumultuous wave of people, all roaring. The Israelites poured into the valley and up the other side, running after the terrified Philistines.

They chased them all the way back to Gath and Ekron. What a battle! What a day! The army of Israel blotted out the ungodly Philistines. It was all thanks to a shepherd boy who dared to answer the challenge of a giant defying Israel and their God.

F. DAVOT

That evening, before David left the valley of Elah, he kneeled down at the very spot where he had killed the giant. He prayed, "Thank You God, for giving victory to Your people!"

David had become a national hero. Rumors about the young giant-killer spread like wildfire throughout the land of Israel. "We want David as our king!" cheered the people as the army triumphantly returned home. This made King Saul even more jealous and angry. He was afraid David would take his kingdom away from him.

But David did not want to fight or hurt Saul. David respected him as the true leader and king of Israel. "Lord God," David prayed, "I pray for peace in our land, and that Saul and I might live in peace."

But this was not possible since there was a war raging inside Saul's own heart. He envied David. He felt threatened by him, and felt he had no choice but to kill his young soldier. He hunted David mercilessly.

David was forced to run away from Saul. Six hundred brave soldiers followed him. "We will help you defeat Saul," they offered. But David was firm. "If God wants to take away the kingdom from Saul," he answered, "He doesn't need our help. We'll wait and see."

David and his six hundred men hid in the wilderness, in caves, and in the small forests of Israel. Once they were forced to hide in a neighboring enemy country. Saul chased them from one end of the land to the other.

One day some terrible news arrived at David's hideout. It hit David like a stunning blow. King Saul was dead!

He had been killed in another great battle against the Philistine army. Many of his sons were dead too. David wept over Saul and his sons. The country was torn apart. Some people remained loyal to Saul's only surviving son. But half the country claimed David as their new king.

F. DAVOT

29

Seven years had passed since David killed Goliath. Another seven years would go by before David became king of a united Israel. What a glorious day that was!

It was not until this day that David realized the importance of what the old prophet Samuel had done so many years ago, when he had anointed him at home in Bethlehem. The anointing had been God's promise that someday He would make David king of Israel.

"Hail the king! Hail King David!" the crowds cheered.

David set up his kingdom in the great city of Jerusalem. He built a magnificent castle right in the center. He conquered the enemies around Israel, and brought the lost Ark of the Covenant back from the land of the Philistines who had captured it long before. David wanted Israel to only worship the one, true God.

David ruled for many years. God made David another promise, "Your kingdom will last forever!"

"How can this be?" wondered David.

One thousand years after David's death, Jesus, the Savior of the world, was born in Bethlehem, the town of David. He was a direct descendant of King David.

Jesus came to establish a kingdom of peace which would have no end. This kingdom lives on even today, within the hearts of those who believe in Him.

You can find the story of David in the Old Testament from the book of 1 Samuel, chapters 16 to 31, and in the book of 2 Samuel.